MAD LIBS  JUNIOR.

SUPER SILLY
MAD LIBS JUNIOR

By Roger Price and Leonard Stern

Mad Libs
An Imprint of Penguin Random House

MAD LIBS
Penguin Young Readers Group
An Imprint of Penguin Random House LLC

Mad Libs format copyright © 2004 by Penguin Random House LLC. All rights reserved.

Concept created by Roger Price & Leonard Stern

Published by Mad Libs,
an imprint of Penguin Random House LLC,
345 Hudson Street, New York, New York 10014.
Printed in the USA.

ISBN 9780843107586
36 34

MAD LIBS JUNIOR INSTRUCTIONS

MAD LIBS JUNIOR® is a game for kids who don't like games!
It can be played by one, two, three, four, or forty.

RIDICULOUSLY SIMPLE DIRECTIONS:

At the top of each page in this book, you will find four columns of words, each headed by a symbol. Each symbol represents a part of speech. The symbols are:

★ **NOUNS** ☺ **ADJECTIVES** → **VERBS** ? **MISC.**

MAD LIBS JUNIOR® is fun to play with friends, but you can also play it by yourself! To begin, look at the story on the page below. When you come to a blank space in the story, look at the symbol that appears underneath. Then find the same symbol on this page and pick a word that appears below the symbol. Put that word in the blank space, and cross out the word, so you don't use it again. Continue doing this throughout the story until you've filled in all the spaces. Finally, read your story aloud and laugh!

EXAMPLE:

"Goodbye!" he said, as he jumped into his _____ and _____
                                                ★   →

off with his pet _____.
                       ?

★ NOUNS	☺ ADJECTIVES	→ VERBS	? MISC.
car	curly	drove	hamster
boat	purple	~~danced~~	dog
roller skate	wet	drank	cat
taxicab	tired	twirled	~~giraffe~~
~~surfboard~~	silly	swam	monkey

e said, as he jumped into his __SURFBOARD__ and __DANCED__
                                     ★   →

t __GIRAFFE__.
        ?

MAD LIBS ☺ JUNIOR.
QUICK REVIEW

In case you haven't learned about the parts of speech yet, here is a quick lesson:

A **NOUN** ★ is the name of a person, place, or thing. *Sidewalk, umbrella, bathtub,* and *roller skates* are nouns.

An **ADJECTIVE** ☺ describes a person, place, or thing. *Lumpy, soft, ugly, messy,* and *short* are adjectives.

A **VERB** ➜ is an action word. *Run, jump,* and *swim* are verbs.

MISC. ? can be any word at all. Some examples of a word that could be miscellaneous are: *nose, monkey, five,* and *blue.*

MAD LIBS JUNIOR® is fun to play with friends, but you can also play it by yourself! To begin, look at the story on the page below. When you come to a blank space in the story, look at the symbol that appears underneath. Then find the same symbol on his page and pick a word that appears below the symbol. Put that word in the blank space, and cross out the word, so you don't use it again. Continue doing this throughout the story until you've filled in all the spaces. Finally, read your story aloud and laugh!

HOW TO MAKE AN ICE-CREAM SUNDAE

★ NOUNS	😊 ADJECTIVES	➡ VERBS	❓ MISC.
pinecones	creamy	squirt	eye
cherries	fresh	melt	elbow
paper clips	fishy	shake	mouth
worms	stinky	scream	nose
nuts	sweet	wiggle	earlobe
sardines	nasty	cry	eyebrow
toenails	crunchy	jump	foot
mushrooms	salty	shiver	fist
rubber bands	furry	bounce	nostril
meatballs	yucky	sneeze	finger
glue	tasty	party	knee
beans	rotten	run	heart

Step 1: Always start by placing two scoops of delicious,

_____ ice cream into a bowl. A good scoop should be

about the size of your _____ ?.

Step 2: Drizzle some hot caramel, chocolate sauce, and a heap of

_____ over the scoops of ice cream. The ice cream may start

to _____ a little, but don't worry.

Step 3: Next, sprinkle on some _____ sprinkles, a great big

squirt of whipped cream, and a handful of _____ . Be creative

and add whatever toppings your _____ desires.

Step 4: Now you're ready to _____ ! Grab a great big

spoonful and shove it into your _____ to see how it tastes.

What a _____ treat!

MAD LIBS JUNIOR® is fun to play with friends, but you can also play it by yourself! To begin, look at the story on the page below. When you come to a blank space in the story, look at the symbol that appears underneath. Then find the same symbol on his page and pick a word that appears below the symbol. Put that word in the blank space, and cross out the word, so you don't use it again. Continue doing this throughout the story until you've filled in all the spaces. Finally, read your story aloud and laugh!

COMIC-BOOK HERO

★	😊	➡	?
NOUNS	**ADJECTIVES**	**VERBS**	**MISC.**
spider	lumpy	laugh	ankle
pirate	sad	shiver	finger
flashlight	hairy	hop	toe
hamster	goofy	shake	arm
pineapple	smelly	dance	bottom
flea	fancy	burp	head
noodle	scary	snore	wrist
house	magical	freeze	lung
elephant	ugly	itch	stomach
balloon	boring	sneeze	thumb
turnip	spiffy	twist	lip
shoe	old	wink	thigh

MAD LIBS JUNIOR.
COMIC-BOOK HERO

My favorite comic-book character is the Purple _____. She's

a superhuman creature with tons of _____ powers. When a

bad guy attacks, her _____ turns into the size of a/an

_____ and shoots out a poison _____.

She is able to make any enemy _____ with fright. Her

sidekick is a giant purple _____ who starts to

_____ whenever he smells trouble. And she rides around

in a/an _____ jet that's shaped like a/an _____.

When she isn't fighting crime, she poses as a/an _____

schoolteacher. The only key to her identity is a/an _____

purple mark right above her _____. When I grow up, I

hope I _____ just like her!

MAD LIBS JUNIOR® is fun to play with friends, but you can also play it by yourself! To begin, look at the story on the page below. When you come to a blank space in the story, look at the symbol that appears underneath. Then find the same symbol on his page and pick a word that appears below the symbol. Put that word in the blank space, and cross out the word, so you don't use it again. Continue doing this throughout the story until you've filled in all the spaces. Finally, read your story aloud and laugh!

SHOPPING FOR SNEAKERS

★ NOUNS	☺ ADJECTIVES	➡ VERBS	? MISC.
lights	ugly	jumping	arm
pumpkins	wet	shopping	foot
holes	smelly	running	eye
lizards	cool	crying	tongue
apples	shiny	falling	ear
parrots	brown	swimming	hand
teddy bears	small	sliding	butt
spaceships	furry	burping	head
footballs	green	dancing	lip
bricks	nasty	diving	stomach
hippos	slimy	drinking	elbow
pickles	funny	rolling	nose

MAD LIBS ☺ JUNIOR.
SHOPPING FOR SNEAKERS

My dad took me to the _____→ mall to buy me a/an

_____ new pair of sneakers. My old ones were too

_____ and they had a/an _____ hole in the toe.

Any time I stepped in a puddle, my _____**?** would get totally

_____ . At the mall, we went to the _____**?**

Shack, where they sell the best _____★ in town. I

picked out a/an _____ pair and tried them on.

I was so excited, I started _____→ right there in the store.

Dad said they made my feet look like _____★ . They were

_____ ! I love my new sneakers and they are great for

_____→ in puddles!

MAD LIBS JUNIOR® is fun to play with friends, but you can also play it by yourself! To begin, look at the story on the page below. When you come to a blank space in the story, look at the symbol that appears underneath. Then find the same symbol on his page and pick a word that appears below the symbol. Put that word in the blank space, and cross out the word, so you don't use it again. Continue doing this throughout the story until you've filled in all the spaces. Finally, read your story aloud and laugh!

AT THE CANDY STORE

★ NOUNS	☺ ADJECTIVES	→ VERBS	? MISC.
ants	crunchy	taste	arm
peanuts	gross	lick	finger
pencils	sweet	punch	mouth
snails	green	bite	belly
toilets	stinky	hug	cheek
sardines	salty	twist	eyelid
treats	chewy	fart	lung
warts	hairy	eat	earlobe
pickles	orange	scrub	nostril
gum balls	sticky	tickle	elbow
turtles	yummy	squeeze	throat
prunes	fat	rub	brain

MAD LIBS JUNIOR.
AT THE CANDY STORE

My favorite store is the _____ Spot candy store. They

have more _____ than you can fit in your

_____ . There are chocolate-covered _____,

tasty jelly beans, and _____ never-ending lollipops. You can

_____ them for hours and they never shrink! One time, I

dared my _____ little brother to stick five super spicy

_____ in his _____ for a full minute. After ten

seconds, he started to _____ and then his face turned all

_____ . My mom got so _____ when she found

out. I wasn't allowed to _____ any kind of _____

for a whole month. Boy, did I learn a/an _____ lesson! Next

time, I'll dare him to put them in his _____ instead.

MAD LIBS JUNIOR® is fun to play with friends, but you can also play it by yourself! To begin, look at the story on the page below. When you come to a blank space in the story, look at the symbol that appears underneath. Then find the same symbol on his page and pick a word that appears below the symbol. Put that word in the blank space, and cross out the word, so you don't use it again. Continue doing this throughout the story until you've filled in all the spaces. Finally, read your story aloud and laugh!

POP STAR

★ NOUNS	☺ ADJECTIVES	→ VERBS	? MISC.
turkey	hot	shake	ear
banana	lame	dance	eye
candle	ugly	talk	leg
hot dog	cool	swim	arm
river	stupid	smell	nostril
donkey	smelly	sing	hand
flower	lucky	jump	foot
sailor	nerdy	study	shoulder
toothpick	silly	wiggle	ankle
robot	pretty	sit	face
gumdrop	fuzzy	wrestle	kneecap
chicken	lazy	eat	pinky

MAD LIBS JUNIOR.
POP STAR

Sammy Sparks is a/an _____ new pop star. Sammy first

became famous on American Super _____ , a show that

looks for _____ new talent. Her hit song "I Want to

_____ Like a _____" just went to #1 on

the _____ charts. You can hardly turn on the TV without

seeing her _____ ! My mom says she looks like a

_____ , but I think she's so _____ and really

knows how to _____ . I want to learn that move

she does when she starts to _____ with her

_____ . My friend went to her concert and she brought a

_____ up on stage to _____ with her. I'd give

my right _____ to be able to do that!

MAD LIBS JUNIOR® is fun to play with friends, but you can also play it by yourself! To begin, look at the story on the page below. When you come to a blank space in the story, look at the symbol that appears underneath. Then find the same symbol on his page and pick a word that appears below the symbol. Put that word in the blank space, and cross out the word, so you don't use it again. Continue doing this throughout the story until you've filled in all the spaces. Finally, read your story aloud and laugh!

PIZZA PARTY

★	☺	→	?
NOUNS	**ADJECTIVES**	**VERBS**	**MISC.**
shoes	salty	burped	eye
mushrooms	sweet	tripped	brain
crickets	stinky	jumped	finger
rocks	fat	flipped	stomach
frog legs	flaky	screamed	mouth
cars	nasty	cried	foot
jellyfish	crunchy	barfed	heart
tin cans	spicy	laughed	ear
strawberries	rubbery	clapped	hand
diamonds	chunky	snorted	toe
tissues	purple	yelled	tooth
lightbulbs	crispy	wiggled	back

MAD LIBS JUNIOR.
PIZZA PARTY

Because we collected the most _____ , our class won a

_____ pizza party. When I got to the cafeteria, my

_____ started to water. I could smell the gooey melted

_____ and hot _____ crust. When I got

inside, I was so excited that I nearly _____ ! We could have

any topping our _____ desired! Mr. Burger, the

_____ gym coach, was serving the pizzas with his

_____ . "Would you like a piece with _____ on

it?" he asked. I _____ and said, "Yes, please!" I ate so much

_____ pizza that I got a major _____ache.

Maybe that slice covered in _____ wasn't such a

_____ idea!

MAD LIBS JUNIOR® is fun to play with friends, but you can also play it by yourself! To begin, look at the story on the page below. When you come to a blank space in the story, look at the symbol that appears underneath. Then find the same symbol on his page and pick a word that appears below the symbol. Put that word in the blank space, and cross out the word, so you don't use it again. Continue doing this throughout the story until you've filled in all the spaces. Finally, read your story aloud and laugh!

MY PET

★	😀	→	?
NOUNS	**ADJECTIVES**	**VERBS**	**MISC.**
turnip	slimy	shake	snout
lamp	furry	burp	tail
monkey	blue	bite	ear
donut	spiky	scream	leg
motorcycle	ugly	jump	tongue
shoe box	shiny	whistle	beak
octopus	stinky	cry	finger
trash can	mushy	dance	paw
meatball	dirty	wiggle	neck
chair	slippery	sneeze	belly
dolphin	stupid	clap	foot
teacup	fluffy	flip	mouth

MAD LIBS JUNIOR.
MY PET

For my birthday, my parents bought me a pet _____. He is ⭐

so cute that I named him _____. He has a really long 😊

_____ and I love to pet his _____ skin. ? 😊

I bought him a/an _____ collar that he wears around his 😊

_____. And I'm teaching him to _____ and to ? ➡️

come when I _____. Every time he does a trick, I say, "Good ➡️

_____!" and feed him a/an _____. Next, I'm ⭐ ⭐

going to teach him to catch a Frisbee in his _____. Every ?

night, he sleeps on a/an _____ right next to my ⭐

_____ bed. And in the morning, he rubs his 😊

_____ on me to wake me up. What a/an ?

_____ pet! 😊

MAD LIBS JUNIOR® is fun to play with friends, but you can also play it by yourself! To begin, look at the story on the page below. When you come to a blank space in the story, look at the symbol that appears underneath. Then find the same symbol on his page and pick a word that appears below the symbol. Put that word in the blank space, and cross out the word, so you don't use it again. Continue doing this throughout the story until you've filled in all the spaces. Finally, read your story aloud and laugh!

A TRIP TO THE DOCTOR

★ NOUNS	☺ ADJECTIVES	→ VERBS	? MISC.
pancake	scaly	jump	lip
shot	hairy	yelp	face
kangaroo	brown	sing	eye
fork	nasty	worry	skin
pillow	funny	fart	mouth
poodle	chubby	cry	chest
telephone	green	flip	throat
carrot	bumpy	faint	stomach
porcupine	squishy	dance	forehead
balloon	red	shake	bottom
chair	itchy	jiggle	knee
straw	smelly	run	tongue

MAD LIBS ☺ JUNIOR.
A TRIP TO THE DOCTOR

The other day, I woke up and my _____ **?** was sore. I looked

in the mirror and started to _____ **➡**. My skin was all

_____ ☺ and there were little _____ ☺ spots all

over it! My dad told me not to _____ **➡** and took me to the

doctor. When we got there, the nurse stuck a _____ ★ into my

_____ **?** to take my temperature. Then she told me to

_____ **➡** for one minute while she got the doctor. The doctor

was a/an _____ ☺ woman with bad breath and a cold

_____ **?** that she pressed on my _____ **?**. She said

I had the worst case of the _____ ★ pox she had ever seen!

MAD LIBS JUNIOR® is fun to play with friends, but you can also play it by yourself! To begin, look at the story on the page below. When you come to a blank space in the story, look at the symbol that appears underneath. Then find the same symbol on his page and pick a word that appears below the symbol. Put that word in the blank space, and cross out the word, so you don't use it again. Continue doing this throughout the story until you've filled in all the spaces. Finally, read your story aloud and laugh!

HOW TO CLEAN YOUR ROOM

★ NOUNS	☺ ADJECTIVES	➡ VERBS	? MISC.
cupcake	silly	smell	hand
sock	dumb	bite	arm
dog	gross	hide	foot
watermelon	slimy	lick	head
wrench	smart	kick	chin
zebra	rotten	push	nose
sausage	nice	rub	lip
helicopter	stinky	poke	ear
toothbrush	horrible	squeeze	neck
lizard	goofy	tickle	eyelid
sandwich	funny	punch	knee
trophy	tasty	squish	belly

MAD LIBS JUNIOR.
HOW TO CLEAN YOUR ROOM

Here are four _____ steps to cleaning your room:

1) Start with the closet. If you open the doors and a _____

doesn't fall on your _____ , the closet is clean.

2) If you find an old _____ lying on the floor, pick it up and

_____ it to see if it's clean. If it smells _____ ,

stick it in a drawer.

3) Make a giant _____ out of all of the _____

clothes lying on the floor. Then cover it up with a large

_____ . Or use your _____ to help you

_____ everything under the bed.

4) Offer to give your little brother a _____ if he cleans

your room. He's probably too _____ to know you

don't mean it!

MAD LIBS JUNIOR® is fun to play with friends, but you can also play it by yourself! To begin, look at the story on the page below. When you come to a blank space in the story, look at the symbol that appears underneath. Then find the same symbol on his page and pick a word that appears below the symbol. Put that word in the blank space, and cross out the word, so you don't use it again. Continue doing this throughout the story until you've filled in all the spaces. Finally, read your story aloud and laugh!

MY BABYSITTER

★ NOUNS	☺ ADJECTIVES	→ VERBS	? MISC.
dump truck	normal	spit	lips
airplane	stupid	jump	eyelashes
hamburger	ugly	burp	ears
elephant	stinky	dance	nostrils
pizza	scary	dribble	hair
submarine	funny	slide	hands
flower	old	fly	ankles
worm	creepy	fart	teeth
cloud	lucky	squirt	fingers
ostrich	pretty	leap	arms
jump rope	silly	wiggle	toenails
iceberg	dorky	snort	knees

MY BABYSITTER

Every Friday, my parents go out to _____ ➡ the night away

and Becky comes over to baby-sit. She's so _____ ! She's in

high school, which means she's really _____ and can drive

a/an _____ ★ . She even has pierced _____ ? , which

Mom says is _____ , but I think it's cool. Becky doesn't

make us follow any _____ rules. She always gets us a/an

_____ ★ for dinner and let's us eat with our _____ ? .

One time, she taught me how to make milk _____ ➡ out of my

_____ ? . She always let's us stay up late watching

_____ movies and she doesn't even make us brush our

_____ ? before bed!

MAD LIBS JUNIOR® is fun to play with friends, but you can also play it by yourself! To begin, look at the story on the page below. When you come to a blank space in the story, look at the symbol that appears underneath. Then find the same symbol on his page and pick a word that appears below the symbol. Put that word in the blank space, and cross out the word, so you don't use it again. Continue doing this throughout the story until you've filled in all the spaces. Finally, read your story aloud and laugh!

VIDEO GAME

★ NOUNS	☺ ADJECTIVES	→ VERBS	? MISC.
squid	stupid	licked	ears
snake	sunken	kissed	hands
alien	dirty	pinched	brains
clam	lucky	kicked	muscles
chicken	fishy	sniffed	eyes
potato	slippery	tickled	legs
lobster	smelly	grabbed	teeth
pirate	ugly	punched	fins
monkey	shiny	hugged	arms
donut	magical	squished	lips
kitten	slimy	trapped	feet
turtle	filthy	smacked	elbows

MAD LIBS ☺ JUNIOR.
VIDEO GAME

My favorite new video game is "Super Sea _____." To win

the game, you have to find the _____ ⊙ treasure in the ship

before you are _____ ➡ by a huge _____ ★ ! I

always choose to be the _____ ★ because he has super

_____ ? that grow each time he eats a/an _____ ★ .

But you can only get those in the _____ ⊙ seaweed forest

that is full of sharks with laser _____ ? . You have to be

really _____ ⊙ to get one. One time, I was _____ ➡

by a giant jellyfish and had to grab him by his _____ ? to

get free. When you win the game, a/an _____ ⊙ mermaid appears

and you ride away on a giant _____ ★ with the treasure.

MAD LIBS JUNIOR® is fun to play with friends, but you can also play it by yourself! To begin, look at the story on the page below. When you come to a blank space in the story, look at the symbol that appears underneath. Then find the same symbol on his page and pick a word that appears below the symbol. Put that word in the blank space, and cross out the word, so you don't use it again. Continue doing this throughout the story until you've filled in all the spaces. Finally, read your story aloud and laugh!

SECRET CLUB

★ NOUNS	🙂 ADJECTIVES	➡ VERBS	? MISC.
newspapers	stinky	eat	arm
cookies	cool	fart	leg
snowmen	gross	sing	ear
boxes	smelly	laugh	eye
sandwiches	slimy	sleep	tongue
toenails	great	dance	shoulder
bananas	slippery	burp	knee
sticks	fun	cry	lip
snails	ugly	sneeze	nose
rocks	stupid	stink	stomach
tires	boring	jump	foot
lizards	fuzzy	scream	elbow

MAD LIBS JUNIOR.
SECRET CLUB

My friends and I started a club called "The Top Secret _____."

We meet after school and eat _____ and talk about

_____ . It's really _____! We made a/an

_____ clubhouse out of old _____ in

my friend's backyard. To enter, you have to know the secret

_____ shake. First, you put your _____

on your _____ and then you _____ . You

also have to say the secret password, "_____ snakes." Our

club has two main rules: 1) No _____ allowed.

2) You can't _____ in the clubhouse. My friend's

_____ bulldog is our club pet—too bad all he does is

_____ . He's so fat, his _____ won't

even fit in the clubhouse!

MAD LIBS JUNIOR® is fun to play with friends, but you can also play it by yourself! To begin, look at the story on the page below. When you come to a blank space in the story, look at the symbol that appears underneath. Then find the same symbol on his page and pick a word that appears below the symbol. Put that word in the blank space, and cross out the word, so you don't use it again. Continue doing this throughout the story until you've filled in all the spaces. Finally, read your story aloud and laugh!

A TRIP TO THE LIBRARY

★ NOUNS	☺ ADJECTIVES	➡ VERBS	? MISC.
pirates	boring	eating	head
hippos	stinky	jumping	ear
wizards	stupid	swimming	finger
dinosaurs	ugly	snoring	hand
grapefruits	hairy	chewing	tongue
frogs	smelly	skating	elbow
apes	silly	sneezing	eyebrow
scientists	short	singing	bottom
kangaroos	beautiful	surfing	ankle
bats	furry	bathing	forehead
goats	exciting	dancing	arm
fairies	funny	sleeping	lip

MAD LIBS JUNIOR.
A TRIP TO THE LIBRARY

I love to go to the _____ library. I get all my favorite books

about _____ that have lots of _____ adventures

_____ in strange lands. My little brother likes _____

books about _____. They used to roam the Earth, but then

the _____ Age came and they all started _____.

Mom said I should check out a book called *Famous* _____

in History, but it sounded really _____. I guess I was

_____ too loudly, because the librarian rushed over,

waving her _____ at me. She's pretty _____!

She has a big _____ and looks kind of like one of those

_____ you'd see _____ in the wild on a

nature show. I grabbed my _____ and left!

MAD LIBS JUNIOR® is fun to play with friends, but you can also play it by yourself! To begin, look at the story on the page below. When you come to a blank space in the story, look at the symbol that appears underneath. Then find the same symbol on his page and pick a word that appears below the symbol. Put that word in the blank space, and cross out the word, so you don't use it again. Continue doing this throughout the story until you've filled in all the spaces. Finally, read your story aloud and laugh!

MONSTER UNDER THE BED

 ★	 😊	 ➡	?
NOUNS	**ADJECTIVES**	**VERBS**	**MISC.**
anteater	furry	lick	nose
lion	slimy	tickle	tongue
dumpling	silly	bite	arm
sock	hairy	hug	leg
pork chop	bumpy	sniff	brain
skateboard	funny	squeeze	lip
lollipop	crazy	grab	toe
hairball	ugly	eat	ear
leaf	scary	chew	tooth
noodle	creepy	rub	snout
gum ball	stupid	poke	mouth
cupcake	smelly	shake	eyelash

MAD LIBS JUNIOR.
MONSTER UNDER THE BED

I told my dad that there was a/an _____ monster living

under my bed. He said that was a/an _____ thing to say and

that it was all in my _____ ? . But I knew the monster looked

like a giant _____ ★ with a really big _____ ? .

One time, I heard him _____ → an old _____ ★

that was under my bed. And if I dangled a/an _____ ? over

the bed, the monster would quickly _____ → it with his long

_____ ? . As soon as Dad turned off the light, there was a/an

_____ noise under the bed! Dad was so scared that he

started to _____ → my arm. But it turned out that the monster

was just my _____ little kitten!

MAD LIBS JUNIOR® is fun to play with friends, but you can also play it by yourself! To begin, look at the story on the page below. When you come to a blank space in the story, look at the symbol that appears underneath. Then find the same symbol on his page and pick a word that appears below the symbol. Put that word in the blank space, and cross out the word, so you don't use it again. Continue doing this throughout the story until you've filled in all the spaces. Finally, read your story aloud and laugh!

MY BEST FRIEND'S HOUSE

★ NOUNS	☺ ADJECTIVES	➡ VERBS	? MISC.
shark	stinky	smell	legs
bucket	fuzzy	bite	lips
gorilla	yummy	hug	fingers
rubber band	giant	tickle	feet
shoe	ugly	see	eyes
toothpick	sticky	pinch	toes
poodle	chubby	wash	knees
mushroom	fizzy	shake	earlobes
backpack	funky	nibble	elbows
monkey	hairy	lick	arms
eggplant	slimy	sniff	nostrils
goldfish	happy	poke	pinkies

MAD LIBS JUNIOR.
MY BEST FRIEND'S HOUSE

My best friend's house is so _____! She has a huge

_____-shaped pool in her backyard. We swim for hours—

until our _____ get all wrinkly! Then we play with her

_____ collection in her big, _____ bedroom.

She also has a pet _____ that lives in a cage in her room.

His name is _____. Sometimes he sticks his _____

through the cage and tries to _____ you. Her mom invited

me to stay for dinner—she was making my favorite fried chicken

_____. She's a really _____ cook. Too

bad I had to go home and clean my _____!

MAD LIBS JUNIOR® is fun to play with friends, but you can also play it by yourself! To begin, look at the story on the page below. When you come to a blank space in the story, look at the symbol that appears underneath. Then find the same symbol on his page and pick a word that appears below the symbol. Put that word in the blank space, and cross out the word, so you don't use it again. Continue doing this throughout the story until you've filled in all the spaces. Finally, read your story aloud and laugh!

AT THE CIRCUS

★	☺	➡	?
NOUNS	**ADJECTIVES**	**VERBS**	**MISC.**
pie	stupid	shake	eye
banana	cool	scream	ear
flower	smelly	jump	nose
meatball	scary	flip	lip
goldfish	boring	cry	belly
trash can	silly	dance	back
octopus	gross	burp	elbow
peanut	ugly	cheer	bottom
sandwich	fun	sneeze	neck
noodle	yucky	juggle	mouth
pillow	stinky	laugh	knee
candy bar	weird	wiggle	toe

MAD LIBS JUNIOR.
AT THE CIRCUS

For a treat, my dad took me to the Big _____ Circus. It sure

⭐

was _____! There was a man who shot himself out of a
😎

huge _____. He wore a helmet on his _____
⭐   ?

to protect himself. When he landed safely on a big _____,
⭐

the whole crowd started to _____. My dad liked the tiger
➡

that would _____ every time its trainer gave it a/an
➡

_____. And at one point, the trainer stuck his
⭐

_____ right in its _____! But my favorite
?   ?

part was when a/an _____ clown with a big red
😎

_____ came over and pulled a/an _____
?   ⭐

out of my _____. I was so excited, I thought I would
?

_____!
➡

MAD LIBS JUNIOR® is fun to play with friends, but you can also play it by yourself! To begin, look at the story on the page below. When you come to a blank space in the story, look at the symbol that appears underneath. Then find the same symbol on his page and pick a word that appears below the symbol. Put that word in the blank space, and cross out the word, so you don't use it again. Continue doing this throughout the story until you've filled in all the spaces. Finally, read your story aloud and laugh!

PLAYING T-BALL

★	☺	→	?
NOUNS	**ADJECTIVES**	**VERBS**	**MISC.**
weasels	ugly	pinched	eye
mice	stinky	rubbed	ear
fleas	stretchy	kicked	back
anteaters	horrible	poked	head
minnows	gross	tickled	leg
squirrels	furry	hit	arm
mushrooms	silly	pushed	nose
puppies	bad	punched	hand
monkeys	nervous	shook	foot
ants	lame	grabbed	elbow
cats	goofy	twisted	ankle
aliens	super	shoved	shoulder

MAD LIBS JUNIOR.
PLAYING T-BALL

This year, I joined a/an _____ league T-ball team. My uniform

is really _____! There's a jersey with our team name, the

Mighty _____ on it, and a pair of _____

pants. My dad also makes me wear _____ pads in case I fall

down. I was really _____ at our first game. I swung the bat

with my _____ as hard as I could. I _____ the

ball, then ran like I was being chased by wild _____.

A group of _____ started cheering. My dad screamed,

"_____ job, slugger!" After the game, the coach

_____ me on the _____ and said I was a really

_____ player!

MAD LIBS JUNIOR® is fun to play with friends, but you can also play it by yourself! To begin, look at the story on the page below. When you come to a blank space in the story, look at the symbol that appears underneath. Then find the same symbol on his page and pick a word that appears below the symbol. Put that word in the blank space, and cross out the word, so you don't use it again. Continue doing this throughout the story until you've filled in all the spaces. Finally, read your story aloud and laugh!

BIRTHDAY PARTY

★ NOUNS	☺ ADJECTIVES	→ VERBS	? MISC.
flounder	stupid	dancing	tooth
watermelon	cool	swinging	arm
chicken	slimy	crying	head
octopus	dumb	jumping	eye
TV	funny	eating	lip
coconut	nasty	swimming	nose
caterpillar	greasy	falling	ear
T-rex	ugly	laughing	mouth
spider	stinky	screaming	tail
truck	furry	singing	ankle
bowling ball	silly	cheering	back
toilet	lumpy	shaking	chin

For my _____ birthday, I had a dinosaur party. The

invitations were _____ .They had a picture of a prehistoric

_____ on them. My mom made _____

tacos and a cake in the shape of a/an _____ . My dad and

I made a/an _____ piñata that looked like a dinosaur

_____ .We stuffed it with candy and a/an _____ as

?

a special prize! All the guests started _____ around the

➡

piñata. Since I was the birthday _____ , I got to go first.

I picked up a/an _____ and started _____

➡

wildly.Too bad I missed the piñata and hit my _____ cousin

right in the _____ !

?

MAD LIBS JUNIOR® is fun to play with friends, but you can also play it by yourself! To begin, look at the story on the page below. When you come to a blank space in the story, look at the symbol that appears underneath. Then find the same symbol on his page and pick a word that appears below the symbol. Put that word in the blank space, and cross out the word, so you don't use it again. Continue doing this throughout the story until you've filled in all the spaces. Finally, read your story aloud and laugh!

MY BIG SISTER

★ NOUNS	☺ ADJECTIVES	→ VERBS	? MISC.
pencils	ugly	snorts	eyes
underwear	nasty	yells	lips
candy bars	awesome	farts	ears
socks	purple	laughs	legs
zits	hairy	coughs	arms
teddy bears	stupid	burps	shoulders
tissues	tacky	screams	nostrils
dentures	slimy	sneezes	ankles
gerbils	silly	sings	elbows
meatballs	puffy	claps	fingers
cotton balls	dumb	cheers	toes
warts	shiny	whistles	eyebrows

MAD LIBS JUNIOR.
MY BIG SISTER

My big sister is really _____  . We look exactly alike, but she

has blue _____ **?** . She also has bigger _____ **?**

than me. She always has tons of _____ makeup smeared all

over her _____ **?** . She's fifteen and has _____ ★

on her teeth to make them _____ . We have to share a/an

_____ room. She always _____ → really loudly

and leaves _____ ★ all over the place for me to clean

up. Whenever I look at her _____ ★ , she gets very

_____ and throws a big fit. Then she _____ →

until her _____ **?** get all _____ . And she says I'm

a brat!

MAD LIBS JUNIOR® is fun to play with friends, but you can also play it by yourself! To begin, look at the story on the page below. When you come to a blank space in the story, look at the symbol that appears underneath. Then find the same symbol on his page and pick a word that appears below the symbol. Put that word in the blank space, and cross out the word, so you don't use it again. Continue doing this throughout the story until you've filled in all the spaces. Finally, read your story aloud and laugh!

GOING OUT TO DINNER

★ NOUNS	😀 ADJECTIVES	➡ VERBS	? MISC.
egg	weird	eat	ear
squid	tasty	poke	eye
tissue	exotic	stab	armpit
pickle	spicy	grab	belly
goat	salty	tickle	knee
octopus	crunchy	sniff	elbow
duck	fresh	lick	mouth
alligator	stinky	steal	nose
eel	nasty	find	nostril
worm	raw	bite	throat
onion	roasted	nibble	stomach
turtle	squishy	wiggle	palm

MAD LIBS JUNIOR.
GOING OUT TO DINNER

My family likes to eat _____ food. The other night, we went

out to dinner to _____ sushi. My favorite thing is a/an

_____ tuna roll. It's pieces of tuna wrapped up with

_____ and rice. My dad likes the spicy _____

roll. It has a whole fried _____ on it! Always use chopsticks

to _____ your sushi. Grab your chopsticks between your

_____ and your _____. It's best to shove the whole

piece in your _____ at once. I like to dip my sushi in

_____ sauce and a/an _____ green paste

called wasabi. My little brother thinks sushi is _____,

so he always gets a bowl of noodles topped with a/an _____

_____.

MAD LIBS JUNIOR® is fun to play with friends, but you can also play it by yourself! To begin, look at the story on the page below. When you come to a blank space in the story, look at the symbol that appears underneath. Then find the same symbol on his page and pick a word that appears below the symbol. Put that word in the blank space, and cross out the word, so you don't use it again. Continue doing this throughout the story until you've filled in all the spaces. Finally, read your story aloud and laugh!

MY NEW SCOOTER

★ NOUNS	😊 ADJECTIVES	➡ VERBS	? MISC.
toilet	shiny	cry	ear
trash can	cheap	laugh	eye
rosebush	furry	scream	nose
giraffe	stupid	dance	pinky
friend	orange	jump	lip
stop sign	ugly	sing	head
pumpkin	chunky	yell	mouth
horse	flimsy	wiggle	chin
dump truck	funky	burp	elbow
family	yellow	giggle	toe
dog	speedy	sneeze	eyelash
mouse	slippery	clap	shoulder

MY NEW SCOOTER

My grandpa bought me a/an _____ new scooter. I can't wait

to show it to my _____ . The wheels on my scooter are really

_____ ! To ride it, you use your _____ to push

off on the ground, and steer with your _____ . The first day I

got it, I rode into a _____ on the street and hurt my

_____ . Grandpa came running as soon as I started to

_____ . Now I have to wear a _____ on my

head and _____ pads. Grandpa says watching me

ride a scooter is like watching a _____ that's trying to

_____ !

Join the millions of Mad Libs fans creating wacky and wonderful stories on our apps!

Download Mad Libs today!